BUILDING SIGHT VOCABULARY: GRADE
TABLE OF CONTENTS

Introduction 2
Word List..3
Assessment 4
Letter to Parents...6

UNIT 1
Lesson 1
  Practice 7
  Story 1: *My Red*  9
Lesson 2
  Practice 11
  Story 2: *A Good* 13
Lesson 3
  Practice 15
  Story 3: *Get in Here* 17
Lesson 4
  Practice 19
  Story 4: *2* 21
Game for Stories 1-4 23
Review for Stories 1-4......................................24

UNIT 2
Lesson 5
  Practice 25
  Story 5: *Go in the* 27
Lesson 6
  Practice 29
  Story 6: *Fun in the Lake*............................31
Lesson 7
  Practice 33
  Story 7: *Fun in a Car*.................................35
Lesson 8
  Practice 37
  Story 8: *Come and Ride* 39
Game for Stories 5-8 41
Review for Stories 5-8......................................42

UNIT 3
Lesson 9
  Practice 43
  Story 9: *Let Me Help!*................................45
Lesson 10
  Practice 47
  Story 10: *Do You Want to Play?* 49

Lesson 11
  Practice 51
  Story 11: *Make a Cake*...............................53
Lesson 12
  Practice 55
  Story 12: *Who Will Run?*...........................57
Game for Stories 9-12 59
Review for Stories 9-12....................................60

UNIT 4
Lesson 13
  Practice 61
  Story 13: *Something for You*......................63
Lesson 14
  Practice 65
  Story 14: *The Ride*......................................67
Lesson 15
  Practice 69
  Story 15: *Up in a Tree*................................71
Lesson 16
  Practice 73
  Story 16: *Work in a Tree* 75
Game for Stories 13-16 77
Review for Stories 13-16..................................78

UNIT 5
Lesson 17
  Practice 79
  Story 17: *Do You Have a* *?*........81
Lesson 18
  Practice 83
  Story 18: *Come See* 85
Lesson 19
  Practice 87
  Story 19: *Run and Jump* 89
Lesson 20
  Practice 91
  Story 20: *Find Little Pony* 93
Review for Stories 17-20..................................95

Answer Key 96

BUILDING SIGHT VOCABULARY: GRADE 1

INTRODUCTION

Sight words are those words which occur most frequently in the English language and often have no content to help the student remember them. Words like *this* and *has* are more difficult to remember than *boat* or *clown* because sight words are not easily linked to a mental picture. A beginning vocabulary is made up almost entirely of sight words.

A large sight vocabulary helps the student read faster. Students who read more quickly feel confident in their skill and will be more likely to read for fun, thus insuring greater practice time. Comprehension is also expanded through the use of sight words. Readers spend less time decoding words and more time focusing on the sentence meaning. Moreover, sight words often provide context clues to further develop important process skills.

ORGANIZATION

Each lesson focuses on four or five sight words. A lesson is comprised of two Practice pages and a story. There are four lessons in each unit. A game and a one-page review are also included in each unit.

Practice Pages: The first Practice page introduces the sight words in Key Sentences. A variety of activities provide practice and reinforce word recognition. Activities include matching, word completion, capitalization, and cloze procedure. The second Practice page reviews the words just taught and those learned in the previous lesson. Activities on this page might include configuration clues, word recognition through letter order, word finds, and sentence context.

Stories: Each story is designed to be copied front to back on a single sheet of paper. Students cut the page in half and staple the halves to make a four-page booklet. The stories are written so that students practice the new sight words in context, as well as review previously taught words. Unfamiliar words are underlined in rebus pictures in the first five

stories. As students' reading skills improve, unfamiliar words are underlined in the story and identified by labels in art. Rebus pictures in the margins of the first ten stories identify the speaker. The remaining stories identify direct discourse by using the speaker's name.

Games: A game accompanies each unit to review the sight words in a fun context. They are to be mounted on construction paper, colored, and cut out. Game pieces can be stored in envelopes for easy management.

Reviews: The last page of each unit reviews words in sentence context. Student recognition and comprehension of the words can be checked at this time.

USE

Determine the implementation that best fits your students' needs. The following plan suggests a format you may wish to use:

On the first day, write the Key Sentence(s) on the board and underline Key Words. Read the sentence(s) several times, pointing to each word. Then have students read the sentence(s) as you point to each word. Give students the first Practice page to complete after providing directions. On the second day, review the Key Sentence(s) and Key Words. Students then complete the second Practice page. On the third day, students prepare the booklets. After reviewing the Key Sentence(s), choral read the story several times. Continue to allow students to practice rereading the story in a variety of settings: in small groups, in pairs, or individually into a tape recorder.

ADDITIONAL FEATURES

Parent Letter Send the Parent Letter home with students.

Assessment An Assessment test is found on pages 4 and 5. You can use the test as a diagnostic tool by administering it before students begin the activities. After they have completed all the lessons, let them retake it to gauge their progress.

Word List

Below is a complete list of the high-frequency words (words that appear on many recognized word lists) that students will master by the end of *Building Sight Vocabulary: Grade I*. The numeral following each word refers to the page on which the word is introduced to students.

A a 11
all 73
am 55
and..................25
are..................47
at 33

B be 83
big 51
blue 15
but..................69

C can 19
come 37

D did 55
do 47
down..............47

F fast.................87
find..................65
for 25
from 69
fun 29

G get 15
give 79
go 19
good................11

H happy.............83
have 11
he 65
help................43

her...................87
here................15

I I 11
in 15
into 91
is 7
it 19

J jump................87
just 83

K know 91

L let 43
like 25
little 33
look 33

M make 51
me..................33
my 7

N not..................7
now 79

O oh...................69
on 37
over...............87

P play 29
put..................79

R red...................7

ride 37
run..................55

S said 51
saw 83
see 11
she 65
so 73
something.......43
stop 69

T that................65
the 25
them...............73
they 61
this 7
to 29

U up..................47
us 61

V very 91

W want 43
was 79
we 29
went 91
what 61
where 61
who 55
will 51
with 37
work 73

Y you 19

© Steck-Vaughn Company

Building Sight Vocabulary 1, SV 6210-5

1. ○ all ○ am ● and	6. ○ if ○ in ○ it	11. ○ did ○ do ○ down	16. ○ for ○ fun ○ run
2. ○ happy ○ help ○ have	7. ○ in ○ is ○ it	12. ○ will ○ with ○ was	17. ○ let ○ like ○ look
3. ○ are ○ at ○ that	8. ○ said ○ this ○ is	13. ○ were ○ we ○ us	18. ○ the ○ that ○ to
4. ○ he ○ her ○ here	9. ○ what ○ you ○ has	14. ○ know ○ little ○ will	19. ○ get ○ good ○ go
5. ○ want ○ who ○ where	10. ○ want ○ was ○ walk	15. ○ blue ○ red ○ did	20. ○ make ○ me ○ my

Assessment
See the Answer Key on page 96 to find which words to read aloud.

Name _____ Date _____

1. ○ on ○ into ○ over	6. ○ big ○ be ○ but	11. ○ jump ○ just ○ up	16. ○ so ○ stop ○ is
2. ○ where ○ will ○ work	7. ○ find ○ for ○ from	12. ○ saw ○ see ○ she	17. ○ said ○ did ○ this
3. ○ have ○ his ○ he	8. ○ ride ○ run ○ red	13. ○ fast ○ find ○ stop	18. ○ them ○ the ○ they
4. ○ play ○ help ○ put	9. ○ we ○ went ○ was	14. ○ are ○ am ○ all	19. ○ make ○ work ○ know
5. ○ her ○ happy ○ help	10. ○ over ○ can ○ come	15. ○ into ○ from ○ over	20. ○ give ○ very ○ jump

Assessment
See the Answer Key on page 96 to see which words to read aloud.

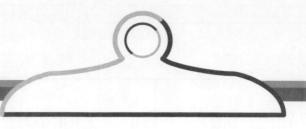

Dear Parent,

Becoming a good reader is a challenge during the primary education years. Children discover how sounds and words form sentences and paragraphs. Building and retaining a strong sight vocabulary is essential to the reading process. Sight words are those words which occur most frequently in the English language and often have no content to help the reader remember them. Recognizing these basic words helps the child read faster and develop strong decoding skills, thus making a better reader.

During the year, your child will be developing sight vocabulary through practice sheets, booklets, and games. After being introduced to four core words, your child will bring home the completed practice sheets and a four-page booklet. Games will also be included at the end of each unit. Your child will progress at a much faster rate if you will consistently review and practice what is brought home. To best help your child, please consider the following suggestions:

- Listen to your child read the new stories several times. Ask questions to help your child understand the meaning of the story.
- Save all the stories. Encourage your child to frequently reread the old stories.
- Together, review practice pages. Have your child read the Key Sentences and Key Words. Then find ways to use those sentences and words frequently.
- Play the new games and practice the new words with your child. Continue to play the old games for review.

Thank you for your help. Your child and I appreciate your assistance and reinforcement in this learning process.

Cordially,

Name _____

Date _____

© Steck-Vaughn Company

This is not my red ○ .

this   is   not   my   red

■ this   is   not   my   red

th_s   '_s   no_t   _y   r_d

t_is   i_   no_   _y   re_

_his   _i_   _ot   _y   _ed

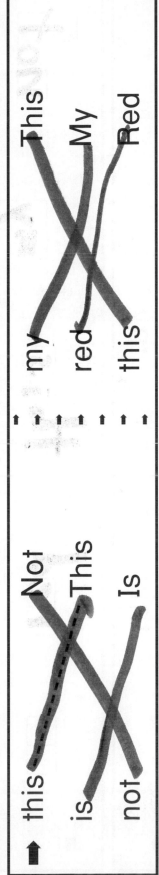

↑ this   is

   This   red   My

   Not   this   Red

   Is   my

   not

◄ 1. This _i_s_ not my red ○ .

   2. This is not _my_ red ○ .

● Students read the Key Sentence, read the words below, and draw a line from each word to the same word in the Key Sentence. ■ Students fill in the missing letters.

■ Students draw lines to match capitalized and lowercase forms of each word. ▲ Students read the sentence and write a Key Word that makes sense in the sentence.

Lesson 1: Practice

Building Sight Vocabulary 1, SV 6210-5

Name _____

Date _____

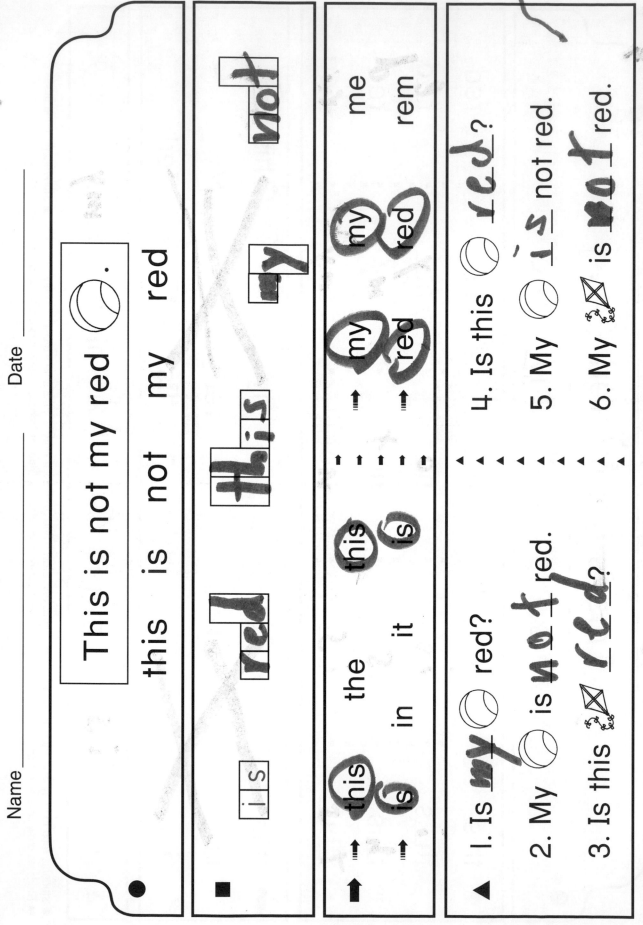

● This is not my red ⊙.

this   is   not   my   red

■ | not |

| my |

| this |

| red |

| i | s |

▲ ↑ this is

↑ the in it

↑ ↑ ↑ ↑

↑ my red

↑ my red

me

rem

▲ 1. Is _my_ ⊙ red?

2. My ⊙ is _not_ red.

3. Is this ⊠ _red_?

▲ 4. Is this ⊙ _red_?

◄ 5. My ⊙ _is_ not red.

◄ 6. My ⊠ is _not_ red.

● Students read the Key Sentence, read the words below, and draw a line from each word to the same word in the Key Sentence. ■ Students count the boxes and find a word with the same number of letters. Have them print a letter in each box. ↑ Students say the word, point to the letter by the arrow, and point to the first letter of the next word to compare the words. ▲ Students read the sentence and write a Key Word that makes sense in the sentence. ▲ Students circle the word. If all letters in both words are the same, they will circle the word.

© Steck-Vaughn Company

8

Lesson 1: Practice
Building Sight Vocabulary 1, SV 6210-5

Name **anilye**

This is my .
My is red.

✂ -

This is red.
This is not my .

2

Is this my ?

My is not red.

anilyse

✂ -

4

This is my .

This is my .

This is not red.

anilyse

© Steck-Vaughn Company

10

Name _____

Date _____

| I have a good 🪁. See? |

I   have   a   good ✗ see

■
have		see
have		see
have		see
have		good
good		good
good		good

→
good	See
a	Good
have	A
see	Have

▲ goodnihaveguzIr(see)bgood

★ 1. I have a red 🚗.

2. See my good 🚗.

3. I have a good 🐱.

* * * * * * * * * * *

4. I have a red 🪐.

5. see my red ☄️.

6. see my red 🪐.

- Students read the Key Sentence, read the words below, and draw a line from each word to the same word in the Key Sentence. ■ Students fill in the missing letters.
↑ Students draw lines to match capitalized and lowercase forms of each word. ▲ Have each student start at the triangle and run a finger below the row of letters until finding a word. Circle each word and read it. ★ Students read the sentence and write a Key Word that makes sense in the sentence.

© Steck-Vaughn Company

11

Lesson 2: Practice
Building Sight Vocabulary 1, SV 6210-5

Name

Date

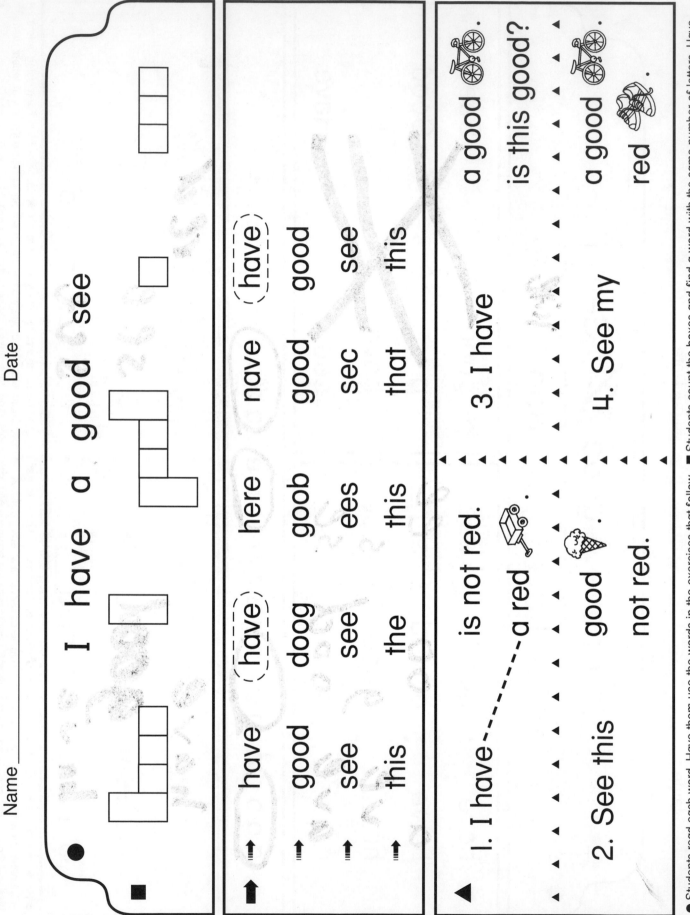

● I have a good see

■

■

↑ have   have   nave

↑ good   doog   goob   good

↑ see   see   ees   sec

↑ this   the   this   that

◀ 1. I have   is not red.

▶ ▶ ▶ ▶ ▶

2. See this   a red

3. I have   a good

good .   is this good?

4. See my   a good

not red.   red .

● Students read each word. Have them use the words in the exercises that follow. ■ Students count the boxes and find a word with the same number of letters. Have them print a letter in each box. ↑ Students circle the words in each row that are the same as the first word in the row. ▲ Students read the sentence stem at the left and the two possible endings. They choose the ending which makes sense and draw a line to connect the two sentence parts.

© Steck-Vaughn Company

12

Lesson 2: Practice
Building Sight Vocabulary 1, SV 6210-5

 See my ?

I have a good .

My is red.

This is a good red .

Name _____

✂ -

 See?

See my good red !

 See this!

I have a good !

3

© Steck-Vaughn Company

Building Sight Vocabulary 1, SV 6210-5

2

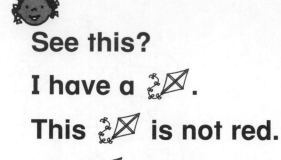

See this?

I have a .

This is not red.

My is good.

4

See my ?

My is a good !

See my ?

My is not good!

© Steck-Vaughn Company

Building Sight Vocabulary 1, SV 6210-5

Get in here, blue.

get   in   here   blue

■ get   in   here   blue

et   i_   h_r   bl__

g__t   __n   he____ue   __er

g____   g____   b__e

↑ get   in   here   blue

In   Here   Get   Blue

▲ e g e(t)m o i n w c h e r e r m b l u e l g e t k

★ 1. _____ is my blue ____.

2. My ____ is _____.

3. _____ in here, blue ____.

* * * * * * * * * * * * * * *

4. Here is my _____.

5. Get _____ my blue ____.

6. _____ is my blue ✏.

● Students read the Key Sentence, read the words below, and draw a line from each word to the same word in the Key Sentence. ■ Students fill in the missing letters.
↑ Students draw lines to match capitalized and lowercase forms of each word. ▲ Have each student start at the triangle and run a finger below the row of letters until finding a word. Circle each word and read it. ★ Students read the sentence and write a Key Word that makes sense in the sentence.

Lesson 3: Practice
Building Sight Vocabulary 1, SV 6210-5

Name _____

Date _____

● get in here blue a have good see

■

get got get tag get
in in is it is
here here here have her
blue blue dlue blow blue

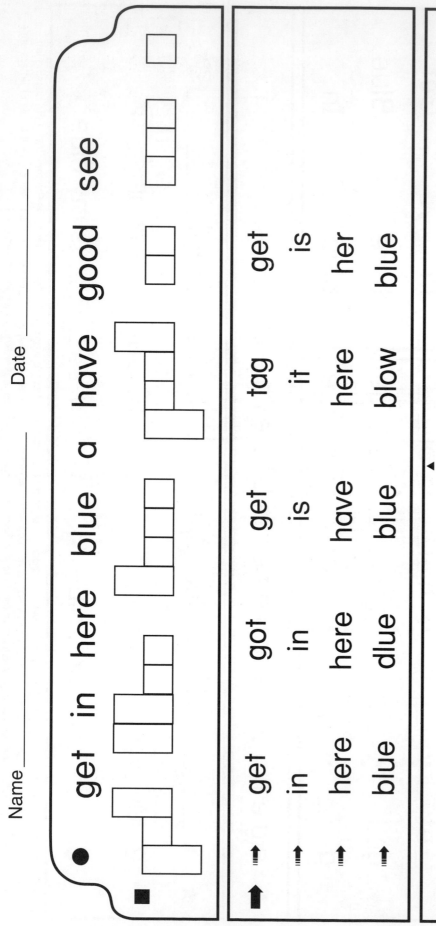

1. Here is   get in.   my blue 🚗.

2. Here is   my blue 🚗.   is this blue?   a red 🚲.

3. Get in   my blue 🚗.

4. Get in   my 🚗.   have a blue 🪐.   the 🪐 blue?

● Students read each word. Have them use the words in the exercises that follow. ■ Students count the boxes and find a word with the same number of letters. Have them print a letter in each box. ➡ Students circle the words in each row that are the same as the first word in the row. ▲ Students read the sentence stem at the left and the two possible endings. They choose the ending which makes sense and draw a line to connect the two sentence parts.

© Steck-Vaughn Company

Lesson 3: Practice
Building Sight Vocabulary 1, SV 6210-5

 I have a good .

See my blue .

My is in here.

Name _____

 -

3

 Here, ! Here, !

See this.

This is good.

Get in here, blue .

2

 See my !

My is not in here.

This is not good.

Get in here, blue !

4

Get in here, blue .

My is in here.

I have a good blue .

© Steck-Vaughn Company

18

Name _____

Date _____

You can go in it.

you   can   go   it

■ you   can   go   it

y_u   c_n   _o   i_

_o   _a   _g   _t

y___   c___   ___   ___

↑ you   Go

can   It

go   You

it   Can

▲ 1. See this good [image].

It can _____.

2. This is my [image].

You can get in _____.

3. My [image] is not good.

It _____ not go.

4. I have a good [image].

_____ can go in it.

● New words are underlined in the Key Sentence. Students read the Key Sentence, read the words below, and draw a line from each word to the same word in the Key Sentence. ■ Students fill in the missing letters. ➡ Students draw lines to match capitalized and lowercase forms of each word. ▲ Students read the sentences and write one of the new words in the blank.

Lesson 4: Practice
Building Sight Vocabulary 1, SV 6210-5

Name _____

● you   can   go   it   get   in   here   blue

■ [boxes for letter printing]

↑

you	you	yon	noy	yes	you
can	cau	nuc	can	can	cat
go	og	go	go	do	good
it	it	it	in	is	it

▲

1. You can   is my [truck] .
                    get in my [truck] .

3. I can   get in it.
                    here it is.

2. You can   go in it.
                    a blue [snake] .

4. It is   in here.
                    can go.

● Students read each word. Have them use the words in the exercises that follow. ■ Students count the boxes and find a word with the same number of letters. Have them print a letter in each box. ↑ Students circle the words in each row that are the same as the first word in the row. ▲ Students read the sentence stem at the left and the two possible endings. They choose which ending makes sense and draw a line to connect the two sentence parts.

20

Lesson 4: Practice
Building Sight Vocabulary 1, SV 6210-5

Here is my 🛒.

It is red.

Can you see this 🛒?

It is not a good 🛒.

Name _____

3

Here, blue !

Go in my red 🛒.

You can go in it.

I can have 2 🦜 🦜
in here.

21

2

You have a good !

Here! You can have

my .

My can not go

in my .

My can go in this .

✂ -

4

See! This is good!

You have a blue

in my .

I have a red in

my .

2   in a —good!

A

I have a red ◯ .

My ◯ is red.

See my good ◯ ?

I have a red ◯ .

Get in here, blue 🐦 .

See my good ◯ ?

Get in here, blue 🐦 .

My ◯ is red.

B

I have a good 🐦 .

See this good 🏠 ?

You can have my 🐦 .

It can go in the 🏠 .

I have a good 🐦 .

It can go in the 🏠 .

See this good 🏠 ?

You can have my 🐦 .

Game for Stories 1-4
Students read all the sentences on side A. Have students cut out the strips, match the sentences that are alike, and paste the two like sentences on a sheet of paper. Repeat the procedure for side B.

Name _____

Date _____

1. I have a _____ [image: truck]

    good   not

2. You can _____ in this [image: birdcage] .

    have   get

3. My [image: ball] is _____ .

    red   go

4. _____ is a good [image: kite] .

    Here   You

5. You can get _____ here, blue [image: bird] .

    it   in

6. Can you _____ this [image: birdcage] ?

    see   my

Students read the sentence and pick the missing word, trace the sentence, and write the missing word on the line.

© Steck-Vaughn Company

Review of Stories 1-4
Building Sight Vocabulary 1, SV 6210-5

Name _____

Date _____

I like red and blue. The 🌂 is for you.

like   and   the   for

like   Like

for   For

and   The

the   And

■
like	and	the	for
L_ke	an_	th_	fo_
li___	a_d	t_e	_or
_ik_	_nd	_h__	f___

▲ 1. The 📖 is red _____ blue.

2. The 🧺 is _____ you.

3. I _____ the 🌸🌸 in here.

4. Here is _____ blue 🎩.

● New words are underlined in the Key Sentences. Students read the Key Sentences. Students read the words below, and draw a line from each word to the same word in the sentences. ■ Students fill in the missing letters. ➡ Students draw lines to match capitalized and lowercase forms of each word. ▲ Students use only the underlined words from the Key Sentences to complete these sentences. Have them write each missing word in the blank.

● and   for   the   like   it   can   go   you

■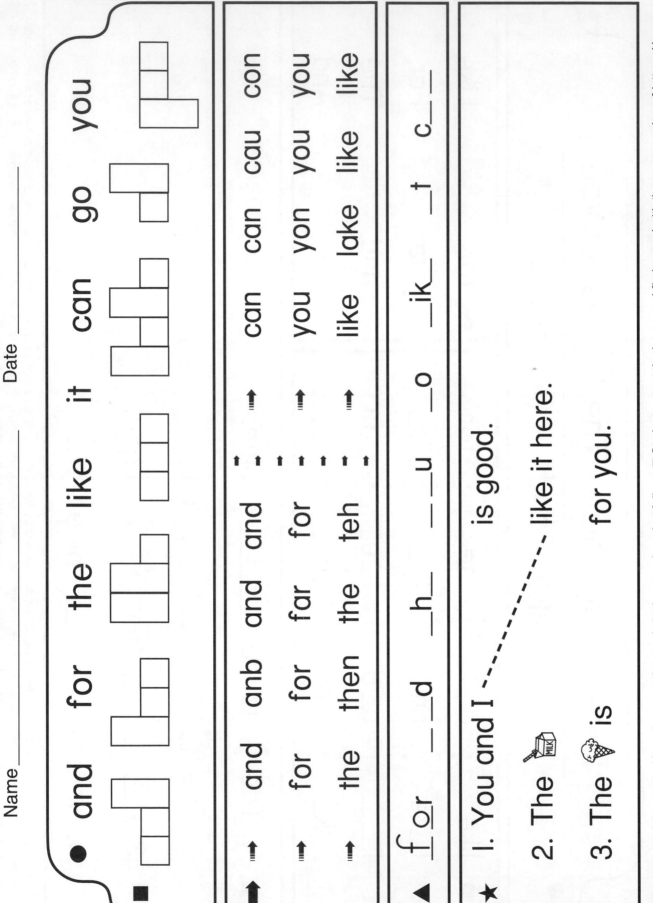

▲ and   anb   and   and   ↑   can   can   cau   con   ↑
  for   for   far   for   ↑   you   yon   you   you   ↑
  the   then   the   teh   ↑   like   lake   like   like   ↑

▲ f o r __ __ d __ h __ __ u __ o __ ik __ __ t c __ __ __

★ 1. You and I ----------- like it here.

   2. The 🥛   is good.

   3. The 🍦 is   for you.

● Students read the words. Have them use the words in the exercises that follow. ■ Students count the boxes and find a word with the same number of letters. Have them print a letter in each box. ➔ Students circle the words in each row that are the same as the first word in the row. ▲ Students count the number of blanks and look at the letter or letters given, then find a word at the top of the page with the same number and positioning of letters. Have them write the missing letters. ★ Students read the sentence stems at the left, read the endings at the right, and draw lines to match the sentence parts.

Name _____

See it . I like .
You and I can go
in the .

Go in the ?
I can not get in the .

✂ -

Here! See this 🌂 .
I have a red and
blue 🌂 .
The 🌂 is for you.
My 🌂 is good for
the .
Can you go like this?

3

© Steck-Vaughn Company
27
Building Sight Vocabulary 1, SV 6210-5

2

You can not go in the ?

The **is for a**  **.**
It is not for a **.**
You get in the **.**
Not I!

4

I like the **.**
I like the red and blue **.**
This **is good for**
    the **.**
Here I go in the **.**
You and I can go
    in the **.**

© Steck-Vaughn Company

Building Sight Vocabulary 1, SV 6210-5

Name _____ Date _____

We like to play and have fun.

we	to	play	fun

fun	Fun
we	We
to	To
play	Play

■
we	to	play	fun
w__	t__	p__ay	__un
__e	__o	__la	f__ __
__ __ __	__ __ __	p__ __y	__u__

▲ 1. We like to have _____ .

2. We can _____ in the 🌳 .

3. It is fun _____ play in the 🌳 .

4. Can _____ play in the 🏫 ?

● New words are underlined in the Key Sentence. Students read the Key Sentence, read the words below, and draw a line from each word to the same word in the Key Sentence. ■ Students fill in the missing letters. ⬆ Students draw lines to match capitalized and lowercase forms of each word. ▲ Students read the sentences and write one of the new words in the blank.

© Steck-Vaughn Company

Lesson 6: Practice
Building Sight Vocabulary 1, SV 6210-5

Name _____

Date _____

■ to we fun play like the for and

↑
_o w__ __o __n t__

__la a__ __i_e t__

◆
het _____ ot _____ ew _____ nda _____ rof _____

keli _____ nuf _____ aply _____ eth _____

★
1. I like to   in the 🛷 .

2. It is fun   play and have fun.

3. We like to play   to play.

● Students read the words. Have them use the words in the exercises that follow. ■ Students count the boxes and find a word with the same number of letters. Have them print a letter in each box. ↑ Students count the number of blanks and look at the letter or letters given, then find a word at the top of the page with the same number and positioning of letters. Have them write the missing letters. ◆ Students unscramble the letters to make one of the Key Words. ★ Students read the sentence stems at the left, read the endings at the right, and draw lines to match the sentence parts.

© Steck-Vaughn Company

30

Lesson 6: Practice
Building Sight Vocabulary 1, SV 6210-5

Name _____

We like to play and
   have fun.
We can go to the <u>lake</u>.

Go to the <u>lake</u>?
We like the <u>lake</u>.
It is fun.

✂ -

This is fun!
I like to play here.
Get in the <u>lake</u>.
It is fun to play in
   the <u>lake</u>.

3

lake

2

We can play in the lake.

Not I!
The lake is not for
a and a .
We can not play in the lake.

 ✂ —

boat

lake

4

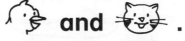
We can not play in the lake.
The lake is not good for
 and .
See this boat?
We can have fun in it.

© Steck-Vaughn Company

32

Building Sight Vocabulary 1, SV 6210-5

Name _____

Date _____

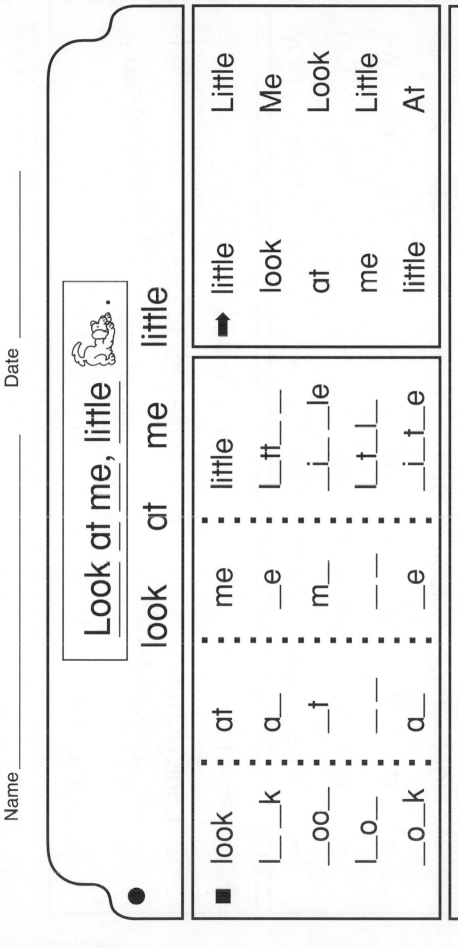

Look at me, little

look   at   me   little

little	Little
look	Me
at	Look
me	Little
little	At

■

look	at	me	little
l__k	a__t	l__tt__e	L__tt__
__oo__	__t	__e	__i__ __le
L__o__		m__	L__t__l
__o__k	a__	__e	__i__t__e

▲
1. Go and get the little ○ for _____.

2. I have a little ○ _____ my ⬛.

3. Go and _____ for my ○.

4. Is this the _____ ○?

● New words are underlined in the Key Sentence. Students read the Key Sentence, read the words below, and draw a line from each word to the same word in the Key Sentence. ■ Students fill in the missing letters. ➡ Students draw lines to match capitalized and lowercase forms of each word. ▲ Students read the sentences and write one of the new words in the blank.

Lesson 7: Practice
Building Sight Vocabulary 1, SV 6210-5

Name _____

Date _____

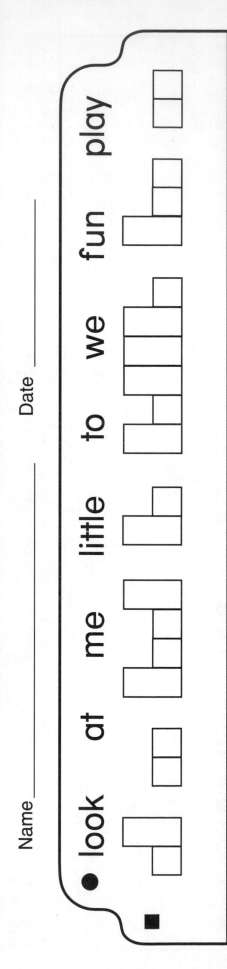

● look   at   me   little   to   we   fun   play

■

↑ look   kool   look   look   ↑ to   at   to   to

↑ at   it   ta   at   all   ↑ we   we   wo   we

↑ me   me   we   em   me   ↑ fun   fnu   fun

↑ little title little litle   ↑ play   paly   play

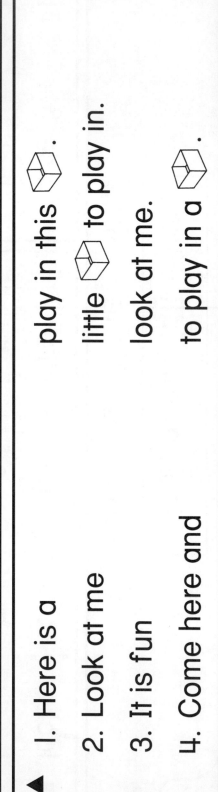

▲ 1. Here is a   play in this ◇ .

2. Look at me   little ◇ to play in.

3. It is fun   look at me.

4. Come here and   to play in a ◇ .

● Students read each word. Have them use the words in the exercises that follow. ■ Students count the boxes and find a word with the same number of letters. Have them print a letter in each box. ➡ Students circle the words in each row that are the same as the first word in the row. ▲ Students read the sentence stems at the left, read the endings at the right, and draw lines to match the sentence parts.

© Steck-Vaughn Company

34

Fun in the <u>Car</u>

Look at this little
   blue <u>car</u>!
Is this little <u>car</u>
   for me?
Can I have this <u>car</u>?
Blue is good for a <u>car</u>.
I like to look at it.

Name _____

✂ —

It is fun. I like it.
I can have fun in it.
Look at me!
Look at me go!
I like to play in my
   little <u>car</u>.
Look at me, little

2

Look at this, .
This is for the little car.
Get in the little car.
Is it fun to play in
    a car?

✂ -

4

Look at this little
    car go.
Look at me go!
This is a good car.
This little car is fun!

Name _____

Date _____

Come on and ride with me.

come   on   ride   with

■ | come | on | ride | with
| c_m_ | _n | r__e | th_
| _o_e | o_ | _id | w__h
| co__ | __ | r_d | w_t

→ ride — — — — — rides

come   likes

look   looks

like   comes

▲ 1. Can you _____ here?

2. I have this 🚲 to ride _____.

3. Ride _____ me.

4. Look at me _____ on this 🚲.

● New words are underlined in the Key Sentence. Read the Key Sentence, read the words below, and draw a line from each word to the same word in the sentence.
■ Students fill in the missing letters. → This exercise adds the inflected ending -s to verbs. Students draw a line to match the root word with its -s form and underline the root word in the right column. ▲ Use only the underlined words from the Key Sentence to complete these sentences. Write each missing word in the blank.

Lesson 8: Practice
Building Sight Vocabulary 1, SV 6210-5

Name _____

Date _____

● come   ride   on   with   look   at   me   little

■ [boxes for spelling practice]

↑ on ⊙n come _____ with _____ ride _____

◀ o_   a_   e_   _th   _m   l_k   _i_e

★ 1. Look at my 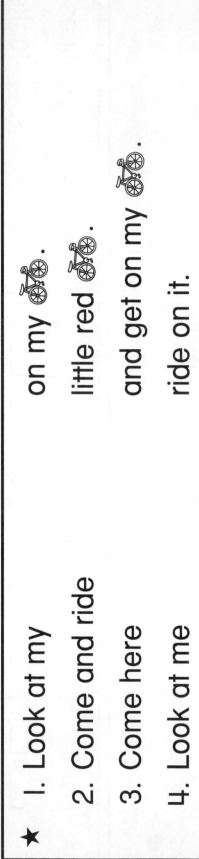 on my 🚲.

   2. Come and ride little red 🚲.

   3. Come here and get on my 🚲.

   4. Look at me ride on it.

● Students read the words. Have them use the words in the exercises that follow. ■ Students count the boxes and find a word with the same number of letters. Have them print a letter in each box. ➡ Students write each word again, beginning it with a capital letter. ▲ Students count the blanks and look at the letter or letters given, then find a word at the top of the page with the same number and position of letters. ★ Students read the sentence stems at the left, read the endings at the right, and draw lines to match sentence parts.

Lesson 8: Practice

Name _____

! ! Here
we come.
Look at my <u>car</u> go.
Come on and ride
with me.
Come on! Get in!
We can go for a ride
in my <u>car</u>.

✂ –

3

We have to get the
<u>wagons</u>.
The <u>car</u> is little.
We can not ride in it.
You and I can play
with the <u>wagons</u>.
Come with me to
get the <u>wagons</u>.

© Steck-Vaughn Company

Building Sight Vocabulary 1, SV 6210-5

2

We can not ride
   with you.
You can ride in the car.
Look! We can not
   get in.
I can get my wagons
and ride.
Come on, .
Ride with me.

- -

4

Look at this!
Can the car go with
   the wagons on it?

Get in and we can see.
Here we go. Come on,
   little car.
See! The little car
   can go!

we

like

look

me

come

ride

at

little

on

with

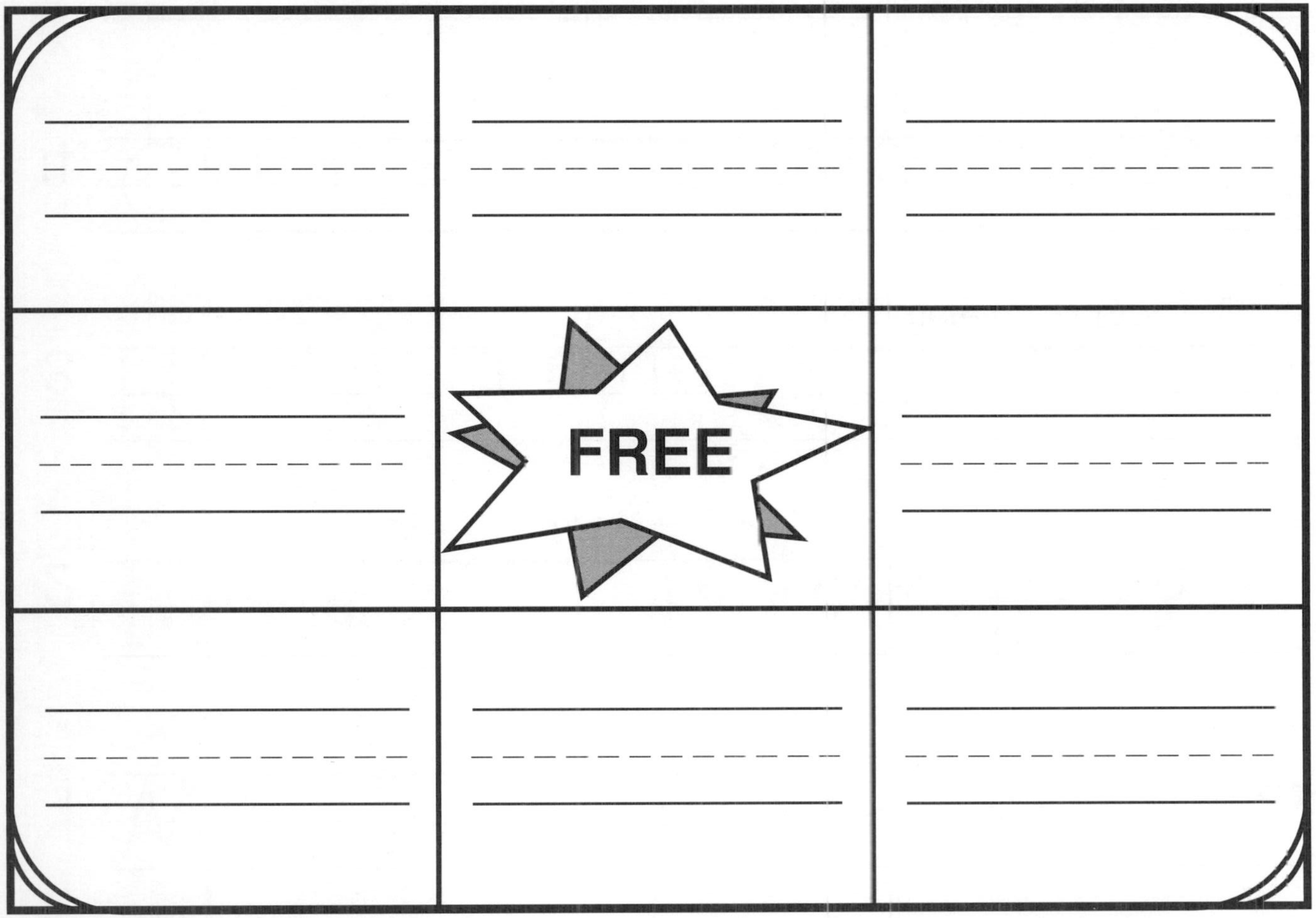

play

fun

to

and

for

the

FREE

Students choose eight words and write them onto the game board squares in any order. They cut out the game board and paste it onto construction paper and then cut out the word cards. As a class or in small groups, students play bingo.

Name _____

Date _____

1. We _____ to play in the _____. 

   like   fun

2. It is _____ to play here.

   fun   for

3. Here is a blue ⊘ _____ you.

   here   for

4. Come _____ and ride with me.

   on   at

5. It is fun to _____ in.

   fun   ride

6. You and I can have fun _____ it.

   with   look

Students will read the sentence and pick the missing word, trace the sentence, and write the missing word on the line.

Review of Stories 5-8
Building Sight Vocabulary 1, SV 6210-5

Name _____

I want something.   Let me help you.

something   want   let   help

■ something

so___th___g

s___et___ng

___me___in___

■ want

w___t

___an___

w___n

■ let

let

___t

___et

___ ___

■ help

help

___el___

h___ ___p

h___ ___

➔ 1. I see something I _____.

2. I like to _____ you.

3. You have _____ good.

4. _____ me ride with you.

● New words are underlined in the Key Sentences. Students read the words below, and draw a line from each word to the same word in the sentences. ■ Students fill in the missing letters. ➡ Students read the sentences and write one of the new words in the blank.

Name _____

Date _____

● something   want   let   help

come   ride   on   with

■

➤ want   went   want   ➔on

➤ help   hlep   help   ➔let   let   tel   lel

➤ come   come   came   come   ➔with   whit   with

▲
1. Here is something   with it?

2. Can you help me   I want.

3. I want   to ride on the 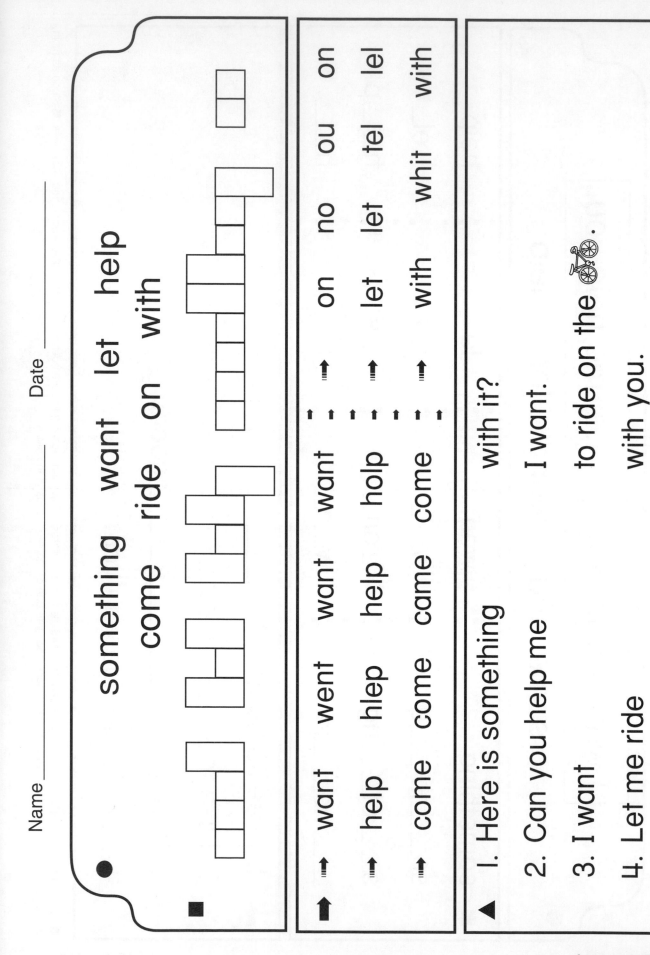.

4. Let me ride   with you.

● Students read each word. Have them use the words in the exercises that follow. ■ Students count the boxes and find a word with the same number of letters. Have them print a letter in each box. ➔ Students circle the words in each row that are the same as the first word in the row. ▲ Students read the sentence stems at the left, read the endings at the right, and draw lines to match the sentence parts.

© Steck-Vaughn Company

Lesson 9: Practice
Building Sight Vocabulary 1, SV 6210-5

I see something I want.

I see berries on a bush.

The berries look good.

Let me get the good red berries.

I can not get to the bush.

Name _____

✂ -

3

I want something.

Look at this apple.

I want it.

I can not get it.

Can you help me?

Can you get the apple for me?

© Steck-Vaughn Company

Building Sight Vocabulary 1, SV 6210-5

2

You see something
   you want.
Let me help you.
I can help.
I can get the <u>berries</u>
   for you.
Here! This is for you.

✂ -

4

You see something
   you want.
Let me help you get it.
Here you go. Can you
   get the <u>apple</u> you want?
This is fun. I help you
   and you help me to get
   something we want.

© Steck-Vaughn Company

Building Sight Vocabulary 1, SV 6210-5

Name _____

Date _____

You are up.	Do you want down?

are   up   do   down

■

are	up	do	down
_re	u_	_o	_ow_
a_e	_p	d_	d__n
a__	___	__	d_w_

do → doing

look   looking

play   playing

go   going

▲ 1. You _____ playing on the 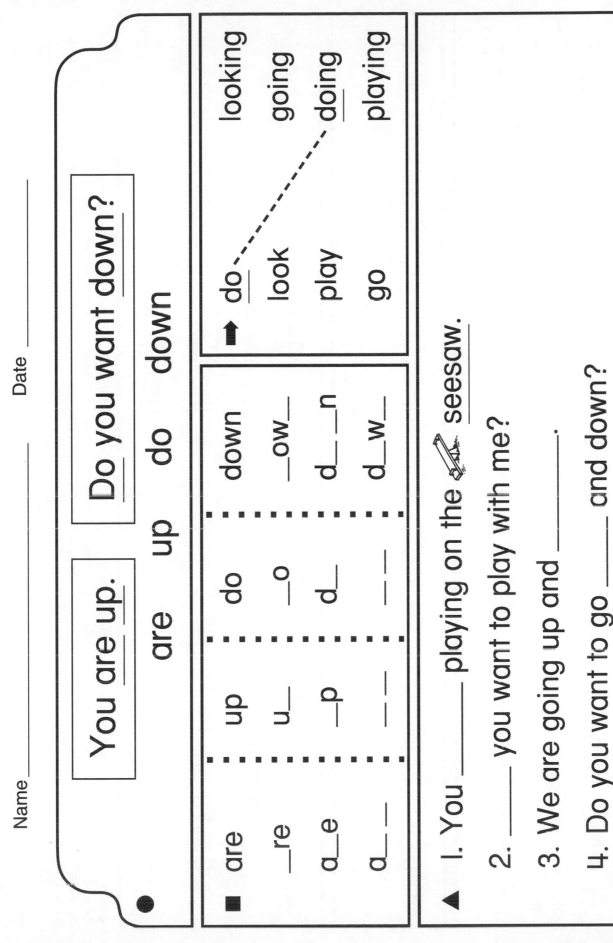 seesaw.

2. _____ you want to play with me?

3. We are going up and _____.

4. Do you want to go _____ and down?

● New words are underlined in the Key Sentences. Students read the Key Sentences, read the words below, and draw a line from each word to the same word in the sentences. ■ Students fill in the missing letters. ➡ This exercise adds the inflected ending -ing to verbs. Students draw a line to match the root word with its -ing form and underline the root word in both columns. ▲ Sentences 1 and 3 contain -ing inflected forms to give students practice reading the words in context. Have students circle these words with -ing after they finish writing the missing words in the sentences.

© Steck-Vaughn Company

Lesson 10: Practice
Building Sight Vocabulary 1, SV 6210-5

Name _____

Date _____

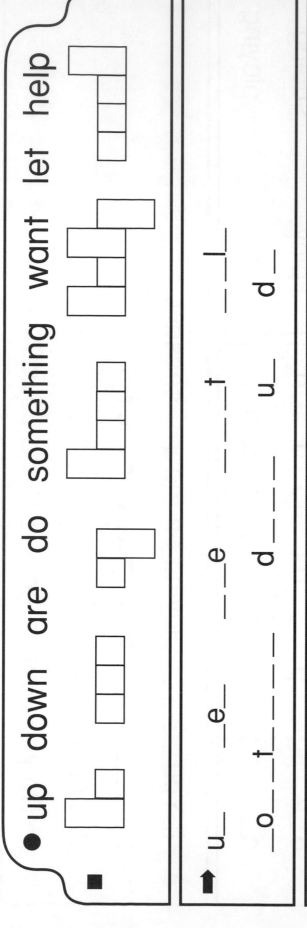

● up down are do something want let help

■

↑ u __ __ e __ __ e __ __ t __ __ l

o __ t __ __ __ __ d __ __ __ __ u __ d __

▲ 1. You are playing   up and down.

2. We are in   on my 🚲.

3. We are looking   the 🍂.

4. I can   help you.

● Students read each word. Have them use the words in the exercises that follow. ■ Students count the boxes and find a word with the same number of letters. Have them print a letter in each box. ➡ Students count the number of blanks and look at the letter or letters given, then find a word at the top of the page with the same number and positioning of letters. Have them write the missing letters. ▲ Students read the sentence stems at the left, read the endings at the right, and draw lines to match the sentence parts.

Name _____

We are going to play in here.
Do you want to play
  with <u>Fox</u> and me?
We have something to play in.
Do you want to play?

Let me see.

✂ -

3

We have something good
  for you.
You are up. Come on down.

We can not get down.
You come up. We are looking
  for help.
Can you help <u>Fox</u> and me
  get down?

2

We like playing this.
Let me get something
   you want.
Do you want something good?
We are going down to get it.

We are going to get
   something you want.
Here we go!

branch

4

Do you want down?
I can help you get down.
Here I come up.
Let me get on the <u>branch</u>.
I can get it to go down.
You can ride down on it
   with me.

© Steck-Vaughn Company

Building Sight Vocabulary 1, SV 6210-5

Name _____

Date _____

I said, "We will make something big."

| said | will | make | big |

■

said	will	make	big
s__d	__il	m__k	b___
__ai__	w__l	__a_e	__ig
s__i__	__i___	m___e	b__g

↑
go	playing
go	going
play	
do	going
go	doing

▲

1. We are playing on something _____.

2. I said, "I _____ make something big."

3. Are you going to _____ this go down?

4. "Make it big," I _____.

● New words are underlined in the Key Sentences. Students read the Key Sentences, read the words below, and draw a line from each word to the same word in the sentences. ■ Students fill in the missing letters. → This exercise adds the inflected ending -ing to verbs. Students draw a line to match the root word with its -ing form and underline the root word in both columns. ▲ Sentences 1 and 3 contain -ing inflected forms to give students practice reading the words in context. Have students circle these words with -ing after they finish writing the missing words in the sentences.

© Steck-Vaughn Company

Lesson 11: Practice
Building Sight Vocabulary 1, SV 6210-5

Name _____

Date _____

● said   will   make   big   up   down   are   do

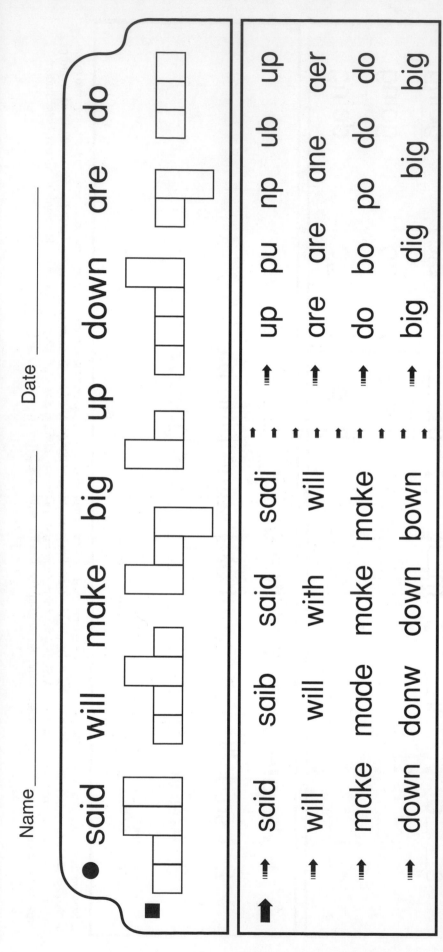

■

→ said   saib   said   sadi   ↑↑↑↑↑↑↑   → up   pu   np   ub   up

→ will   will   with   ↑   → are   are   ane   aer

→ make   made   make   make   → do   bo   po   do   do

→ down   donw   down   bown   → big   dig   big   big   big

▲   1. I said,   it go up and down?

      2. Will you make   make a 🎂 cake.

      3. We will not   this big 🕯 candle?

      4. Do you want   "I will make it."

● Students read each word. Have them use the words in the exercises that follow. ■ Students count the boxes and find a word with the same number of letters. Have them print a letter in each box. → Students circle the words in each row that are the same as the first word in the row. ▲ Students read the sentence stems at the left, read the endings at the right, and draw lines to match the sentence parts.

© Steck-Vaughn Company

Lesson 11: Practice
Building Sight Vocabulary 1, SV 6210-5

Fox said, "Bear, look! This is <u>Rabbit's</u> <u>birthday</u>. Will you make something big?"

<u>Bear</u> said, "I will make a big <u>cake</u> for <u>Rabbit</u>. I will let you help me make it."

Name _____

✂ -

Fox said, "Look at me, <u>Bear</u>. I will make the <u>cake</u> for you. The <u>cake</u> is going in the <u>bowl</u>. The <u>eggs</u> are going in the <u>bowl</u>."

<u>Bear</u> said, "You are going to make a good <u>cake</u>, Fox."

3

© Steck-Vaughn Company

53

bowls

Bear

eggs

milk

2

Bear said, "I will get the big bowls down. The bowls are up here. You can get the milk for me."

Fox said, "Do you want the eggs? Here are the eggs."

✂ —

cake

Bear

pans

4

Bear said, "You are a big help. The cake will go in the pans. And the pans will go in the oven. Rabbit will like this cake."

© Steck-Vaughn Company

Building Sight Vocabulary 1, SV 6210-5

Name _____

Date _____

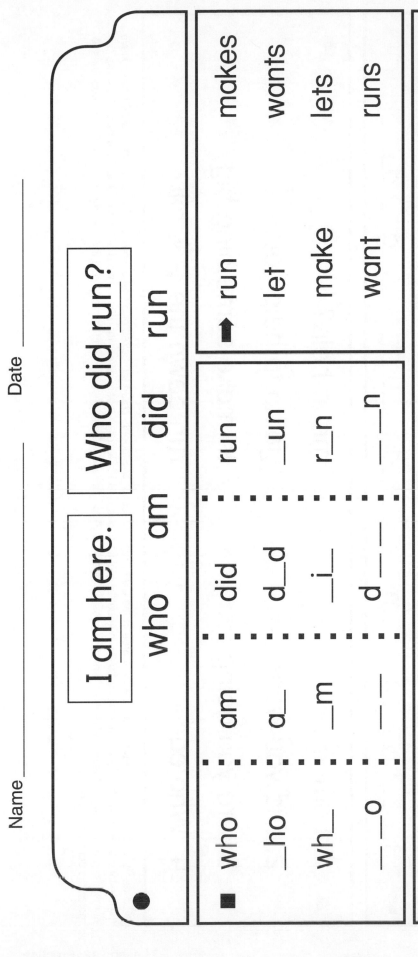

I am here.   Who did run?

who   am   did   run

■
who   am   did   run
_ho   a_   d_d   _un
wh_   _m   _i_   r_n
__o   __   d__   __n

▲ 1. I _____ not see you.

2. _____ will make it for me?

3. Who can _____ up and down the 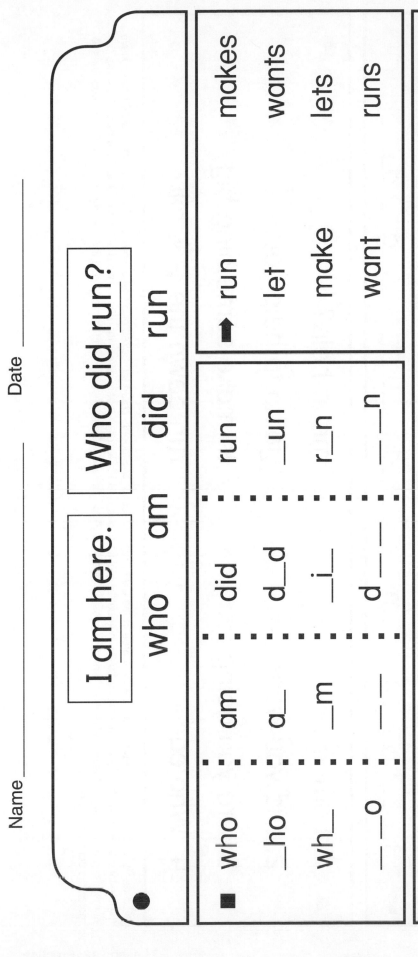 hill?

4. I _____ big and you are little.

run   makes
let   wants
make   lets
want   runs

● New words are underlined in the Key Sentences. Students read the Key Sentences, read the words below, and draw a line from each word to the same word in the sentences. ■ Students fill in the missing letters. ➡ This exercise adds the inflected ending -s. Students draw a line to match the root word with its -s form and underline the root word in both columns. ▲ Use only the underlined words to complete these sentences.

© Steck-Vaughn Company

Lesson 12: Practice
Building Sight Vocabulary 1, SV 6210-5

Name _____

Date _____

● who   am   did   run   will   make   said   big

■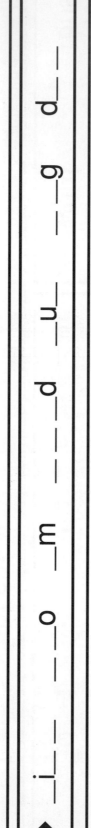

↑   i __ __ o __ m __ __ __ d __ __ u __ __ g d __ __

▲

1. I am   me to help?

2. Did you want   going to help you.

3. Are you going   to make something big?

4. Who can   run down the 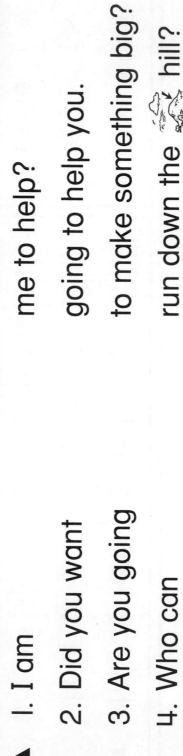 hill?

● Students read each word. Have them use the words in the exercises that follow. ■ Students count the boxes and find a word with the same number of letters. Have them print a letter in each box. ➔ Students count the number of blanks and look at the letter or letters given, then find a word at the top of the page with the same number and positioning of letters. Have them write the missing letters. ▲ Students read the sentence stems at the left, read the endings at the right, and draw lines to match the sentence parts.

© Steck-Vaughn Company

Lesson 12: Practice
Building Sight Vocabulary 1, SV 6210-5

Bear said, "Who is at the door? Did you get it, Fox?"

Fox said, "I am here, Bear. I did get it. Come in, Rabbit."

Rabbit said, "Here I am with something for Squirrel."

Name _____

✂ -

3

Fox said, "This is fun. We have to run to the fence. Who can play this?"

Bear said, "Cat will run with Rabbit."

Rabbit said, "We will see who can get to the fence."

© Steck-Vaughn Company

57

Building Sight Vocabulary 1, SV 6210-5

Squirrel

2

Squirrel said, "Is this for me?"

Rabbit said, "It is for you. It is something to ride. Do you like this? Can you ride it?"

Squirrel said, "I am big. I am not little. I can ride it."

- -

Squirrel

Cat

4

Rabbit said, "Get up, Cat. Get up and run. We can make it. Run!"

Cat said, "Look. We did not see Squirrel. Look at Squirrel run. Run, Squirrel, run!"

And who did run?

Squirrel said, "I did run. I am the winner."

up	do	down	big
up	do	down	big
said	will	make	something
said	will	make	something
want	am	let	are
want	am	let	are
who	help	did	run
who	help	did	run

Game for Stories 9-12

Students will paste the whole page onto construction paper and then cut out the word cards along the dotted lines. To play the game, students will turn the cards face down, then take turns finding pairs of cards that are identical to make matches.

Name _____

Date _____

1. I see something I ____ .
    want   down

2. We ____ going to ride in it.
    at   are

3. ____ me get on my little .
    Help   Want

4. Look at me ____ in the .
    up   do

5. Will you ____ with me?
    make   run

6. You ____ let me ride on it.
    did   are

Students read the sentence and pick the missing word, trace the sentence, and write the missing word on the line.

© Steck-Vaughn Company

Review of Stories 9-12
Building Sight Vocabulary 1, SV 6210-5

What did they make us?

what   they   us

Where is it?

where

■

what	they	us	where
w_a_	t__y	__s	w__er_
_h_t	_h_y	u_	__h_re
__at	t_e_	___	wh____

↑

do	playing
go	doing
play	looking
look	going

▲

1. _____ are you going to do?

2. _____ do you want to go?

3. Are they playing with _____?

4. Are _____ in the 🐦 cage?

● New words are underlined in the Key Sentences. Students read the Key Sentences. ■ Students fill in the missing letters. ↑ This exercise adds the inflected ending -ing to verbs. Students draw a line to match the root word with its -ing form and underline the root word in both columns. ▲ Sentences 1 and 3 contain -ing inflected forms to give students practice reading the words in context. Have students circle these words with -ing after they finish writing the missing words in the sentences.

Name _____

Date _____

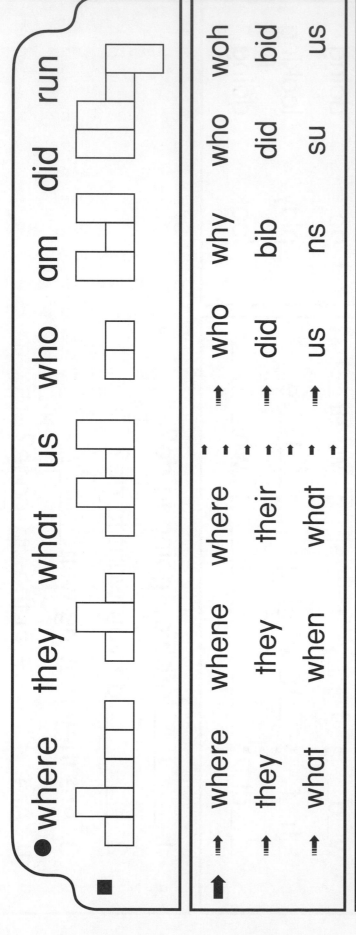

● where   they   what   us   who   am   did   run

■ [letter boxes]

▲

↑ where   ↑ whene   ↑ where   ↑ who   why   who   woh

↑ they   ↑ they   ↑ their   ↑ did   bib   did   bid

↑ what   ↑ when   ↑ what   ↑ us   ns   su   us

▲   1. Where are   looking at us.

      2. They are not   they are going.

      3. What are   you going?

      4. Look where   you doing here?

● Students read each word. Have them use the words in the exercises that follow. ■ Students count the boxes and find a word with the same number of letters. Have them print a letter in each box. ↑ Students circle the words in each row that are the same as the first word in the row. ▲ Students read the sentence stems at the left, read the endings at the right, and draw lines to match the sentence parts.

Lesson 13: Practice
Building Sight Vocabulary 1, SV 6210-5

Nat said, "I see a truck. We can go for a ride. We can ride in the big red and blue truck. What fun we can have!"

"I want to play," said Eric. "I want to have fun. We can make the truck run. We can make it get us where we want to go. This is a good truck for us!"

Name _____

✂ -

3

Nat said, "Look, Jenny and Kim. Look at this truck. We can make the truck go."

Jenny said, "We have something for you. We have something you will like. It will go with the truck."

"Where is it? Did you make it? What did you make for us?" said Eric.

Kim said, "We will get it. We will get what we made."

2

Nat said, "Look at us go! We can make this big truck run. Where do you want to go? Who do you want to see?"

"I see Jenny and Kim. Make the truck go to Jenny and Kim. They will play with us," said Eric.

✂ -

4

Nat said, "What did they make us? What did they make for the truck? Where is it?"

Eric said, "Look, Nat. Look what they did. This truck will have gas. Gas will make this truck run."

Jenny said, "Can we play? We want to have fun in the truck."

Nat said, "Get in. We can go for a big ride."

© Steck-Vaughn Company

Name _____

Date _____

Did she find that?	What did he find?

she   find   that   he

■

he	whehechen
she	shemasher
find	ifinddufindr
that	thethatthat

■

she	find	that	he
_he	f__d	t_a_	_e
sh_	_in_	th__	h_
s_e	f_n_	__at	__

▲

1. We will _____ something that helps us.

2. _____ can find it for you.

3. That is what _____ looks like.

4. _____ is what she wants.

● New words are underlined in the Key Sentences. Students read the Key Sentences, read the words below, and draw a line from each word to the same word in the sentences. ■ Students fill in the missing letters. ➡ Each student starts with the first word and runs a finger below the row of letters. Have them draw circles around the words they find. ▲ Have students circle the words that have -s endings in sentences 1, 3, and 4 after they write the missing words in the blanks.

Lesson 14: Practice
Building Sight Vocabulary 1, SV 6210-5

Name _____

Date _____

■ ● he she find that where they what us

↑ he _____ find _____ she _____ that _____

◄ h _____ t __ t i _____ t __ y u __ e w __ __ __

★ find where it is.

1. Did he find

2. She can   what he wants?

3. Help us   he will find.

4. That is what   go where they are.

● Students read the words. Have them use the words in the exercises that follow. ■ Students count the boxes and find a word with the same number of letters. Have them print a letter in each box. ↑ Students write each word again, beginning it with a capital letter. ◄ Students count the blanks and look at the letter or letters given, then find a word at the top of the page with the same number and position of letters. ★ Students read the sentence stems at the left, read the endings at the right, and draw lines to match sentence parts.

© Steck-Vaughn Company

66

Lesson 14: Practice
Building Sight Vocabulary 1, SV 6210-5

"Here we go. Here we go for a ride. What fun this is!" said Nat.

Jenny said, "Look where you are going, Nat. Do you see what you are doing? Do you see where the truck is going?"

Nat did not look. He did not see the ramp. Down, down, down they go.

Name _____

3

"Here come Jenny and Eric. They have something to help. Look at Eric. What did he find?" said Nat.

Kim said, "Look at Jenny. Did she find that block?"

Jenny and Eric make a seesaw.

"Get on the board," Eric said. "The seesaw will go down with us. The board will make the truck go up."

2

"Look at us. Look where we are. Nat! Nat! You did not look," they said.

Nat said, "My! My! Look what I did. This ride is not for us. We need to find help. Who can we find to help us?"

Eric said, "I will find help. I will find something to get the truck up. Come with me, Jenny. Will you help me?"

"I will help you," said Jenny. "We will find something to get the truck up."

- -

4

Eric said, "What can we find? Where can we find something that will help? Look what I see! I see a board. A board will help get the truck up."

"I see something," said Jenny. "I see a block. That will get the truck up. A board and a block will get the truck up."

Down, down, down they go.

"See the truck go up?" they said. "Good for us. Look at the truck. It is up."

© Steck-Vaughn Company

Building Sight Vocabulary 1, SV 6210-5

Name _____

Date _____

© Steck-Vaughn Company

Oh, stop!	But where did that come from?

oh   stop   but   from

---

oh	stop	but	from
o__	st__	b__t	fr__ __
__h	__op	__ut	__om
__ __	s__ __p	b__ __	f__ __m

→ come	coming
have	having
make	making
ride	riding

▲ 1. Look at it _____ do not stop.

2. This ___ gift for you is _____ me.

3. He wants to _____ coming here.

4. _____, are they riding with us?

● New words are underlined in the Key Sentences. Read the Key Sentences. Read the words below, and draw a line from each word to the same word in the sentences.
■ Students fill in the missing letters. → Students will read the word *come*, mark out the silent *e* in the left column, and read the word *coming* with -*ing* added. Have them underline the -*ing* ending. Repeat the steps for the other words. ▲ Have students circle the words that end with -*ing* in sentences 3 and 4, after they write the missing words in the sentences.

Lesson 15: Practice
Building Sight Vocabulary 1, SV 6210-5

Name _____

Date _____

● oh stop but from he she find that

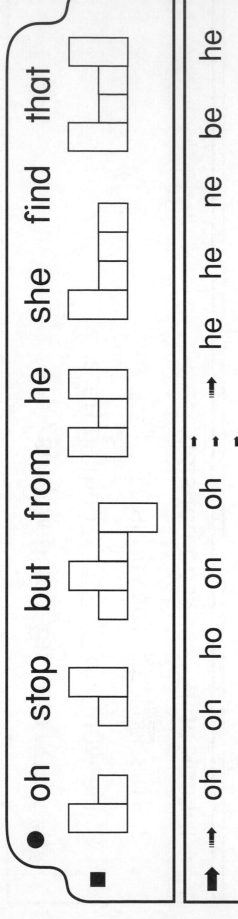

■

→ oh oh ho on oh ↑ he he ne be he

→ stop stop post stop ↑ she she esh she

→ but dut but tub ↑ from for form from

◀ ho _____ tbu _____ mrof _____ pots _____

★ 1. She can   wants to find.

   2. We do not   want to stop here.

   3. That is what he   not find it.

● Students read the words. Have them use the words in the exercises that follow. ■ Students count the boxes and find a word with the same number of letters. Have them print a letter in each box. → Students unscramble the letters to make one of the Key Words. ↑ Have students circle the word with an -s ending in sentence 3 after they match the sentence parts.

© Steck-Vaughn Company

70

Lesson 15: Practice
Building Sight Vocabulary 1, SV 6210-5

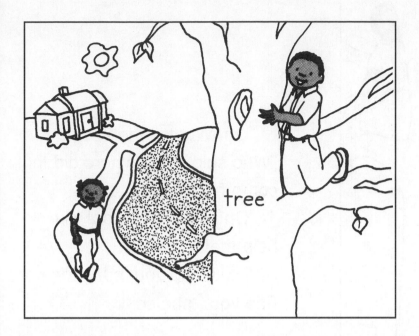

tree

Name_____

"Here I am up this <u>tree</u>, and I will have fun. Here comes Kim, but she can not see me from where she is," said Nat.

"Oh! Stop! Stop! Help!" he said from the <u>tree</u>.

- -

tree

3

"Who is that?" said Kim. "Where are you? Where is that coming from?"

"Look up here in the <u>tree</u>," said Nat.

"Oh, I can see you from here, but you do not want help. You are having fun with me," she said.

"Oh! What is that?" said Kim. "Who said that? Where did that come from?"

"Oh! Stop! Oh, stop! Kim, help me!" said Nat.

"I will help you, but I can not find you," she said.

2

✂ -

"What can you see from up where you are?" said Kim.

Nat said, "Oh, come up and look. You will like what you see from up here."

4

Name _____

Date _____

● | Let them work so you can all play. |

them   work   so   all

them   work   so   all

■ | them   so   all |
| th___   ___o   ___ll |
| _he___   s___   al___ |
| ___em   ___rk   ___l |

■ | work |

↑ | So |
| Them |
| All |
| Work |

them
work
so
all

▲ 1. Look at _____ work.

2. We will work _____ we can play.

3. You will find that _____ is fun.

4. We can _____ go with you.

● Students read the Key Sentence, read the words below, and draw a line from each word to the same word in the Key Sentence. ■ Students fill in the missing letters.
↑ Students draw lines to match capitalized and lowercase forms of each word. ▲ Students read the sentence and write a Key Word that makes sense in the sentence.

© Steck-Vaughn Company

Lesson 16: Practice
Building Sight Vocabulary 1, SV 6210-5

Name _____

Date _____

● them   work   so   all   oh   stop   but   from

■

➡ them _____   all _____   work _____   so _____

◀ _h _ _   _ r _ _   _ _ l _ _   _ _ r _ o   _ _ h _ _   _ _ u

★ 1. Oh, do not   that from us?

2. He wants to stop,   stop here.

3. Did he get   but he can not.

4. Who is going   to work with them?

● Students read the words. Have them use the words in the exercises that follow. ■ Students count the boxes and find a word with the same number of letters. Have them print a letter in each box. ➡ Students write each word again, beginning it with a capital letter. ◀ Students count the blanks and look at the letter or letters given, then find a word at the top of the page with the same number and position of letters. ★ Students read the sentence stems at the left, read the endings at the right, and draw lines to match sentence parts.

© Steck-Vaughn Company

Lesson 16: Practice

Building Sight Vocabulary 1, SV 6210-5

house

tree

"So this is what it looks like from up here. Oh, this is so good! Look at all you can see from up here. Oh, I like to play up in this <u>tree</u>," Kim said.

"We can make a <u>house</u> in this <u>tree</u>," said Nat.

Name_____

✂ -

wood

"I will work up here, and you can help me," Nat said to them. "We will all work so we can have a good <u>tree house</u>."

"Kim, can you get me all that <u>wood</u>?" said Nat.

Kim said, "OK. This is work but it is fun."

Nat said, "I will find something to get the <u>wood</u> up. Will you help me, Tony?"

"OK. Eric and I will work with you." Tony said.

3

© Steck-Vaughn Company

Building Sight Vocabulary 1, SV 6210-5

tree

2

"What fun! But that is work! Can we do all that work?" said Kim.

"I see Tony and Eric from here. We can get them so they can help us. We can all work on it," said Nat.

"We are going to make something in the <u>tree</u>. Do you want to work with us?" Nat said to them.

"Oh, let us help," they said.

Kim said, "Let them work so we can all play."

tree

4

"We like to help you work. We like to work like this. Up, up, up. Look at it go up. Nat can do all the work in the <u>tree</u>. We will work down here," they said.

"What a good <u>tree house</u> we will have," said Nat.

"It is fun to put up something like this," said Tony. "It will give us something good to play in."

© Steck-Vaughn Company

Building Sight Vocabulary 1, SV 6210-5

Name _____

Date _____

Game for Stories 13-16
Students will paste the page onto construction paper and cut out the dominoes along the dotted lines. The first player will match two words end to end and read the matching word. The next player matches a word that has been played and reads the word.

them	from	oh	them	so	all	but
all	so	but	oh	work	from	oh
find	but	they	she	find	where	he
work	them	work	us	os	them	all
stop	they	stop	they	he	where	what
she	where	find	what	stop	stop	she
they	from	where	us	that	he	that
find	that	what	stop	that	work	us

© Steck-Vaughn Company

Game for Stories 13-16
Building Sight Vocabulary 1, SV 6210-5

Name _____

1. Where did she find _____?

    that   they

2. What will they want _____ to do?

    us   up

3. _____ are going up and down.

    Where They

4. I am doing _____ she said.

    what   that

5. _____, what can we do to help?

    Oh   All

6. He is little _____ he can work.

    did   but

Students read the sentence and pick the missing word, trace the sentence, and write the missing word on the line.

78

Review of Stories 13-16
Building Sight Vocabulary 1, SV 6210-5

Give it to me now!

The 🌼 was put in a 🏺.

give   now   was   put

■

give	now	put	was
_i_e	n_w	p_t	_as
gi__	_o_	_u_	w_s
__ve	n___	pu__	_a_

help — helped
look — looked
work — worked
play — played

▲

1. I _____ something in a 🧺 box.

2. He helped you _____ it to them.

3. It _____ so big.

4. We all worked, so _____ we can play.

● New words are underlined in the Key Sentences. Read the Key Sentences, read the words below, and draw a line from each word to the same word in the sentences.
■ Students fill in the missing letters. ➡ Students draw a line to match the root word with its -ed form and underline the root word in both columns. ▲ Have students circle the words that end in -ed in sentences 2 and 4 after they finish writing the missing words in the blanks.

● give was now put them work all so

■

◻◻◻ ◻◻ ◻◻◻ ◻◻ ◻◻◻ ◻◻◻

↑ give gave give good ↑ put but put
↑ was was saw was ↑ now won now how

▲ 1. This 🌸 flower _____   to work now.

2. Put them   was from them.

3. Can I give   you something good?

4. We can not   I put this down?

5. Where can   stop working now.

● Students read each word. Have them use the words in the exercises that follow. ■ Students count the boxes and find a word with the same number of letters. Have them print a letter in each box. ← Students circle the words in each row that are the same as the first word in the row. ▲ Students read the sentence stems at the left, read the endings at the right, and draw lines to match the sentence parts.

Lesson 17: Practice
Building Sight Vocabulary 1, SV 6210-5

"Look at my <u>garden</u>," said <u>Pig</u>. "It is big. Do you want to help me, <u>Duck</u>?"

"I will help you. What can I do?" said <u>Duck</u>.

<u>Pig</u> said, "Get a . You can put a 🌸 in it. We can put the 🌸 in the <u>house</u>."

So, <u>Duck</u> looks for a .

Name_____

 -

3

<u>Duck</u> said, "Now I will go see <u>Kitty</u>. <u>Kitty</u> will have a ."

<u>Duck</u> sees <u>Kitty</u>.

"Oh, <u>Kitty</u>," said <u>Duck</u>, "I want something to put a 🌸 in. Do you have a ? Can you give me a to put a flower in?"

"I will find a now and give it to you. It is good to put a 🌸 in. They will look good," said <u>Kitty</u>.

2

Duck said, "Where can I find a 🏺? Who will give me a 🏺 to put a 🌷 in? I will go see Rooster. He will have a 🏺. Rooster will give a 🏺 to me."

But Rooster did not have a 🏺. He did not give a 🏺 to Duck.

4

Duck said, "Pig! Pig! I have a 🏺 to put the 🌷 in."

"Give it to me now!" said Pig. "A 🌷 will look good in this 🏺."

The 🌷 was put in the 🏺.

"Oh, it looks good," they said. "This 🏺 is good for a 🌷."

© Steck-Vaughn Company

Building Sight Vocabulary 1, SV 6210-5

Name _____

Date _____

You will be happy.   You just saw something.

| just | be | happy | saw |

➔ Be	saw
Just	happy
Happy	be
Saw	just

■

just	be	happy	saw
us__	b__	ha__y	s__w
j__t	__e	__pp__	__aw
__u__t	__ __	h__p__	s__ __

▲ 1. He wants you to be _____.

2. She _____ red and blue 🌸 flowers.

3. _____ give it to me.

4. Who can _____ happy now?

● New words are underlined in the Key Sentences. Students read the Key Sentences, read the words below, and draw a line from each word to the same word in the sentences. ➔ Students fill in the missing letters. ■ Students draw lines to match capitalized and lowercase forms of each word. ▲ Students use only the underlined words from the Key Sentences to complete these sentences. Have them write each missing word in the blank.

© Steck-Vaughn Company

Lesson 18: Practice
Building Sight Vocabulary 1, SV 6210-5

Name _____

Date _____

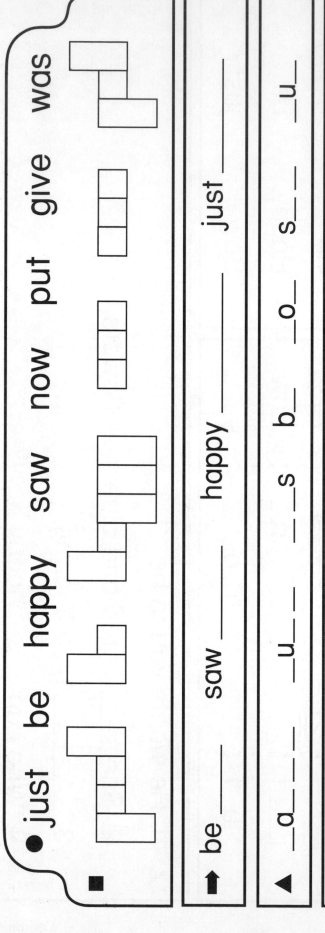

● just be happy saw now put give was

■ [boxes for spelling exercise]

↑ be ____   saw ____   happy ____   just ____

◀ a __ __ __   u __ __   s __ __ __   o __ __   s __ __ u

★ 1. Now put this   to work with you.

2. We will be happy   ride down the 🐦 hill.

3. Give us a   them stop.

4. We just saw   in the ⬡ box.

84

● Students read the words. Have them use the words in the exercises that follow. ■ Students count the boxes and find a word with the same number of letters. Have them print a letter in each box. ➡ Students write each word again, beginning it with a capital letter. ▲ Students count the blanks and look at the letter or letters given, then find a word at the top of the page with the same number and position of letters. ★ Students read the sentence stems at the left, read the endings at the right, and draw lines to match sentence parts.

© Steck-Vaughn Company

Lesson 18: Practice
Building Sight Vocabulary 1, SV 6210-5

"Duck! Come here!" said Pig.

"What do you want?" said Duck.

"I have just come from the barn. I just saw something that you will want to see. It was something good. You will be happy. Come see it," said Pig.

Name_____

3

"You just saw something? What can it be?" said Chick.

"What did you just find in the barn that will make us happy?" they said.

"Come with me, and you can see what I saw," said Pig.

So they all go to the barn.

© Steck-Vaughn Company

85

"Stop! Stop! What is all this? What can be going on?" said <u>Chick</u>.

"I was at the <u>barn</u> just now. I just saw something that will make you happy," said <u>Pig</u>.

2

✂ —

"This is what I saw. I saw this little <u>pony</u>. Just to look at it makes me happy," said <u>Pig</u>.

"Oh, look at the little <u>pony</u>. She makes us all happy," they all said.

4

© Steck-Vaughn Company

Building Sight Vocabulary 1, SV 6210-5

Name _____

Date _____

● We can jump over.   Look at her run fast.

jump over   jump over her fast

■
jump	jumpumjump
over	overcoverv
her	thermoather
fast	stfastfastas

↑
(run)	jump →	want →
(runs)	jumps →	wants →
(running)	jumping →	wanting →
	jumped →	wanted →

▲ 1. I wanted _____ to come here.

2. He runs and jumps _____ the ⬦ box.

3. She and I are running _____ .

4. Where are you going to _____ ?

● *New* words are underlined in the Key Sentences. Students read the Key Sentences. Students read the words below, and draw a line from each word to the same word in the sentences. ■ Students run their finger below each row of letters until finding the word written at the front of the row. Have them draw circles around the words they find. ↑ Have students read the words (*run, runs, running*) and circle each root word. Repeat for the other two columns. ▲ Have students circle the words with *-s*, *-ed*, and *-ing* endings in the sentences after they write the missing words in the blanks.

Name _____

Date _____

● jump over her fast just be happy saw

■ [boxes with letter-shaped squares]

↑ jump just jump jump → her here her
↑ over over own ever → fast first fast far

▲ 1. I saw you   here fast.

2. Give her just   over it fast.

3. She jumped   jump over the ◇ box.

4. Come over   what she wants.

● Students read the words. Have them use the words in the exercises that follow. ■ Students count the boxes and find a word with the same number of letters. Have them print a letter in each box. → Students circle the words in each row that are the same as the first word in the row. ▲ Students read the sentence stems at the left, read the endings at the right, and draw lines to match the sentence parts.

© Steck-Vaughn Company

Lesson 19: Practice
Building Sight Vocabulary 1, SV 6210-5

Duck said, "I am happy that Little Pony can play with us. We will go over to the field where we can let her run and jump. Do not go fast. She is just a little pony. We are big, so we have to help her."

Name_____

3

Little Pony wanted to run fast with them.

"Look at her run fast. We can not run that fast!" said Duck.

"Little Pony! Do not run so fast. Come here with us!" they said.

2

"See this <u>field</u>, <u>Little Pony</u>. We play over here. But look! Over here is a <u>creek</u>. Do not go here. We do not want you to get in the <u>creek</u>. We are big. We can jump over. But you are so little. You can not do that! Let us go play. We will run over to the <u>creek</u> with you. Come on. We will go fast," said <u>Kitty</u>.

4

They saw her running. She was running to the <u>creek</u>. She was not going to stop.

"She is going to the <u>creek</u>. Oh! Stop her! Look at her! She jumped over it!"

Name _____

Date _____

I know it is very big.

I went into the 🌳🌳 .
went   into   know   very

■

went	into	know	very
w__t	i__t	k__w	__er__
__en__	nt__	k__o	v__ __y
w__n__	i__o	__n__w	__e__y

→

doing	jumping
going	looking
finding	helping
wanting	playing

▲

1. I know she went _____ the 🌳🌳 woods.

2. Do you _____ where she is playing?

3. I am working _____ fast.

4. He _____ over to see them.

● New words are underlined in the Key Sentences. Students read the Key Sentences, read the words below, and draw a line from each word to the same word in the sentences. ■ Students fill in the missing letters. → Students will read each word and circle the root word. ▲ Have students circle the words that end with -ing in sentences 2 and 3 after they write the missing words in the blanks.

© Steck-Vaughn Company

Lesson 20: Practice
Building Sight Vocabulary 1, SV 6210-5

Name _____

Date _____

■

● went into know very jump over her fast

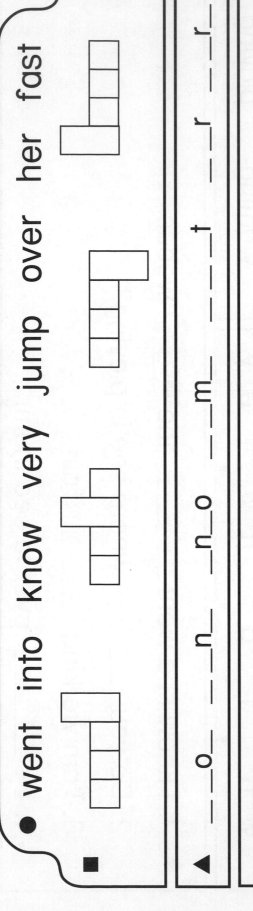

▲ o _ _ _ n _ n_o _ _ m _ _ _ t _ _ r _ _ r _

↑ (looked) wanted worked jumped

jumped helped looked wanted

▲ 1. I know he jumped over this 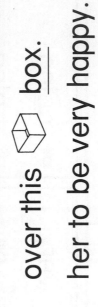 box. ___

2. I know you wanted her to be very happy.

3. She looked into the 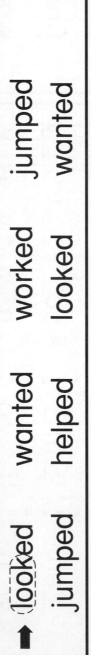 hill fast. ___

4. They went up  box with me. ___

● Students read each word. Have them use the word in the exercises that follow. ■ Students count the boxes and find a word with the same number of letters. Have them print a letter in each box. ↑ Students circle the root words. ▲ Have students circle the words that end in -ed in sentences 1, 2, and 3 after they match the sentence parts.

© Steck-Vaughn Company

Lesson 20: Practice
Building Sight Vocabulary 1, SV 6210-5

"Come on, run fast!" said Duck. "We have to find Little Pony. We do not know where she went. We will all look for her in the <u>woods</u>. I know it is very big. But we have to find Little Pony."

Name_____

- -

3

"Oh, here comes Little Pony!" said Pig. "Where did you go? We know that you went into the <u>woods</u>. We looked and looked, but we did not know where you went."

"I went into the <u>woods</u>. I wanted to run very fast. I am very happy that you looked for me. You wanted to help me. Now I am going to help you," said Little Pony.

2

"We have looked and looked for Little Pony. We want to help, Duck. But we can not run very fast! We can not run at all!" they said.

"We will stop just a little," said Duck.

✂ -

4

"I am going to give you a ride to the <u>barn</u>. You can get on my <u>back</u>. I will give you a very good ride. You can all ride on my <u>back</u> to the <u>barn</u>," said Little Pony.

And so they did.

1. Now I see what it _____ .

was   where

2. I _____ saw them all working.

give   just

3. I will _____ happy to give it up.

be   but

4. _____ it where they can find it.

From   Put

5. She _____ up and down.

went   now

6. Now we can make _____ happy.

she   her

Students read the sentence and pick the missing word, trace the sentence, and write the missing word on the line.

ANSWER KEY

Page 4 1. and 2. have 3. are 4. here 5. who 6. it 7. is 8. said 9. you 10. want 11. down 12. with 13. we 14. little 15. red 16. for 17. let 18. the 19. get 20. make

Page 5 1. into 2. work 3. his 4. put 5. help 6. but 7. from 8. run 9. went 10. come 11. just 12. she 13. find 14. am 15. over 16. so 17. did 18. they 19. know 20. very

Page 7 1. is 2. my

Page 8 is, not/red, this, my, red/not 1. my 2. not 3. red 4. red 5. is 6. not

Page 11 1. have 2. good 3. have 4. red 5. See 6. See

Page 12 have, I, good, a, see

1. I have a red wagon. 2. See this good ice cream cone. 3. I have a good bike. 4. See my red shoes.

Page 15 1. Here 2. blue 3. Get 4. blue 5. in 6. Here

Page 16 get, blue, here, good, in, see, a

1. Here is my blue wagon 2. Here is a red bike. 3. Get in my blue wagon. 4. Get in my car.

Page 19 1. go 2. it 3. can 4. You

Page 20 can, you, get, go, in, here, blue

1. You can get in my wagon. 2. You can go in it. 3. I can get in it. 4. It is in here.

Page 24 1. good 2. get 3. red 4. Here 5. in 6. see

Page 25 1. and 2. for 3. like 4. the

Page 26 and, for, the, can, like, it, you

for, and, the, you, go, like, it, can

1. You and I like it here. 2. The milk is good. 3. The ice cream cone if for you.

Page 29 1. fun 2. play 3. to 4. we

Page 30 fun/for, we, play, to, for/fun, and, the

to, we, for, fun, the, play, and, like, to

the, to, we, and, for, like, fun, play, the

1. I like to play and have fun. 2. It is fun to play. 3. We like to play in the wagon.

Page 33 1. me 2. at 3. look 4. little

Page 34 at, me, look, to, little, fun, me/we

1. Here is a little box to play in. 2. Look at me play in this box. 3. It is fun to play in a box. 4. Come here and look at me.

Page 37 1. come 2. on 3. with

4. ride

Page 38 ride, on, with, look, at, come

on, at, me, with, come, look, ride

1. Look at my little red bike. 2. Come and ride on my bike. 3. Come here and get on my bike. 4. Look at me ride on it.

Page 42 1. like 2. fun 3. for 4. on 5. ride 6. with

Page 43 1. want 2. help 3. something 4. Let

Page 44 want, let, help, something, on

1. Here is something I want. 2. Can you help me with it? 3. I want to ride on the bike. 4. Let me ride with you.

Page 47 1. are 2. Do 3. down 4. up

Page 48 do, are, up, down, help, want

up, let, are, want, help, something, down, up, do

1. You are playing on my bike. 2. We are in the shade. 3. We are looking up and down. 4. I can help you.

Page 51 1. big 2. will 3. make 4. said

Page 52 will, make, big, do, said, up, are

1. I said, "I will make it." 2. Will you make it go up and down? 3. We will not make a cake. 4. Do you want this big candle?

Page 55 1. did 2. Who 3. run 4. am

Page 56 big, run, did, who, will, make, am

will, who, am, said, run, big, did

1. I am going to help you. 2. Did you want me to help? 3. Are you going to make something big? 4. Who can run down the hill?

Page 60 1. want 2. are 3. Help 4. up 5. run 6. did

Page 61 1. What 2. Where 3. us 4. they

Page 62 where, who, what, us, did, they

1. Where are you going? 2. They are not looking at us. 3. What are you doing here? 4. Look where they are going.

Page 65 1. find 2. He/She 3. he/she 4. That

Page 66 they, he, find, she, what, where

them, that, find, they, us, he, what

1. Did he find what he wants? 2. She can go where they are. 3. Help us find where it is. 4. That is what he will find.

Page 69 1. but 2. from 3. stop 4. Oh

Page 70 he, oh, stop, but, from, find

oh, but, from, stop

1. She can not find it. 2. We do not want to stop here. 3. That is what he wants to find.

Page 73 1. them 2. so 3. work 4. all

Page 74 them, work, so, all, from, stop

them, from , all, work, so, oh, but

1. Oh, do not stop here 2. He wants to stop, but her can not. 3. Did he get that from us? 4. Who is going to work with them?

Page 78 1. that 2. us 3. They 4. what 5. Oh 6. but

Page 79 1. put 2. give 3. was 4. now

Page 80 give, was/now, now/was, put, them, work

1. This flower was from them. 2. Put them to work now. 3. Can I give you something good? 4. We can not stop working now. 5. Where can I put this down?

Page 83 just, be, happy, saw/now, now/saw, put

happy, just, was, be, now, saw, put

1. Now put this in the box. 2. We will be happy to work with you. 3. Give us a ride down the hill. 4. We just saw them stop.

Page 87 1. her 2. over 3. fast 4. jump

Page 88 jump, over, her, fast, just be

jump, her, over, fast

1. I saw you jump over the box. 2. Give her just what she wants. 3. She jumped over it fast. 4. Come over here fast.

Page 91 1. into 2. know 3. very 4. went

Page 92 went, into, very, know

know, went, into, jump, went/fast, her, very

1. I know he jumped over this box. 2. I know you wanted her to be very happy. 3. She looked into me box with me. 4. They went up the hill fast.

Page 95 1. was 2. just 3. be 4. Put 5. went 6. her

© Steck-Vaughn Company

Building Sight Vocabulary 1, SV 6210-5